GREEN FINANCE FOR ASIAN STATE-OWNED ENTERPRISES

AN OPPORTUNITY TO ACCELERATE THE GREEN TRANSITION

JUNE 2023

ASIAN DEVELOPMENT BANK

ADB

Notes:
1. In this publication, "$" refers to United States dollars.
2. ADB recognizes "China" as the People's Republic of China; "Korea" as the Republic of Korea; and "Vietnam" as Viet Nam.

Cover design by Maro de Guzman.

On the cover: State owned enterprises will be crucial to the low-carbon transition in Asia and the Pacific, and green finance can make that transition possible. (All photos are from ADB.)

Contents

Tables, Figures, and Boxes

Acknowledgments

This study was prepared by Christoph Nedopil, consultant, under the supervision of David Robinett and the Asian Development Bank's State-Owned Enterprise Working Group, chaired by Hiranya Mukhopadhyay. The authors would like to thank the following people for their helpful comments and insights: Rafael Abbasov, Giacomo Giannetto, Anjum Israr, Andrew McCartney, and Kosintr Puongsophol.

Abbreviations

ACMF	ASEAN Capital Markets Forum
ADB	Asian Development Bank
ASEAN	Association of Southeast Asian Nations
CBI	Climate Bonds Initiative
COP26	United Nations Climate Change Conference
ESG	environmental, social, and governance
EU	European Union
GBP	Green Bond Principles
GHG	greenhouse gas
ICMA	International Capital Markets Association
JV	joint venture
PPP	public–private partnership
PRC	People's Republic of China
SDG	Sustainable Development Goal
SOE	state-owned enterprise

Executive Summary

The world faces a dual environmental crisis through climate change and biodiversity loss. State-owned enterprises (SOEs) are in a unique position to take a leading role in confronting these challenges and shifting economic activity from polluting to green. This requires a shift in existing business models, particularly in the energy, finance, transport, and water sectors, which in Asia are traditionally dominated by SOEs. This shift requires billions of (United States) dollars in financing, and will unleash investments in green and resilient economies, innovation, and jobs. However, a failure to green SOEs risks climate and natural catastrophes.

To move to the core of the green transition, SOEs can utilize an ever-broader sustainable finance toolbox, which is becoming necessary to reduce government borrowing in tight sovereign debt markets. In particular, green bonds, blue bonds, and transition bonds can become an important source of capital for SOEs in many countries around the world. So far, however, the potential of sustainable finance and, in particular, green bonds for SOEs remains mainly untapped, particularly in the emerging economies of Asia.

This report provides an overview of the role and use of sustainable financial instruments for SOEs in emerging countries of Asia. It shows how SOEs can address specific governance and capacity gaps resulting from their (part) ownership by governments to successfully prepare to access green capital markets.

Five points stand out with regard to the effort to improve SOE governance and green bankability:
  (i)   SOEs need to **establish sound governance systems** in relation to their government owner to give them the permission to raise funds from capital markets and to improve risk management, transparency, and accountability to fulfill basic investor requirements.
  (ii)   SOEs need to establish a **credible green strategy,** with a strong project pipeline to attract investors.
  (iii) SOEs need to **improve the bankability** of their projects and ideally of the whole SOE through improved financial management and operational efficiency to reduce costs and improve delivery as well as cash flows to reduce financial risks for investors.
  (iv)   SOEs need to **build capacity and knowledge on green bond issuance** according to domestic and/or international green bond standards.
  (v)   SOEs need to **build relevant monitoring, reporting, and verification capacity** to provide information in a timely manner on the use of proceeds (or the impact of the sustainable-linked instrument) to investors.

By accelerating the use of green finance, SOEs generate multiple benefits for long-term sustainable development for the SOE itself as well as for the broader economic development (as summarized in the following table).

Benefits of the Use of Green Finance by State-Owned Enterprises

Benefits for SOEs	Benefits for Broader Economic Development
• SOEs can transition from polluting to green business models to provide **long-term economic resilience**. • By utilizing green financial instruments, such as green bonds, SOEs can potentially **lower their financing cost** if they can make use of the "greemium." • By preparing to issue green financial instruments on public markets, SOEs **improve corporate governance**, including risk management, transparency, and information disclosure, to **improve performance and accountability**.	• Accelerating green SOE investments will unleash **green and resilient development opportunities** in the whole economy. • By building more green infrastructure in energy, transport, and other sectors, **green innovation and procurement** are accelerated, providing private sector benefits. • By raising green capital through green financial institutions, SOEs can lead by example. This may help **local capital market development** (e.g., with more capacity of capital markets, verifiers, auditors, underwriters), which then makes it simpler for the private sector to raise money with the right pricing. • Paired with a just transition mechanism to support workers and communities, the green transition can **provide economic, environmental, and social benefits**.

SOE = state-owned enterprise.
Source: Authors.

Beyond reforms to make SOEs more bankable and better able to access green finance, the enabling environment for SOE green finance can also be improved. Specific actions on this include

(i) **improving policy frameworks for the green transition** through road maps and binding regulations (e.g., climate targets), reducing non-green incentives, and supporting the development of carbon pricing —or other policies that help internalize negative externalities, such as emissions—to provide credible signals to private and public companies for future investment directions;

(ii) **addressing real economic barriers for green development**, e.g., through supporting the development of local green manufacturing and research and development capacity;

(iii) **developing local capital market capacity and structures**, including frameworks for green finance and disclosure, that are attractive and trustworthy to international investors;

(iv) **improving SOE governance and management** from the regulator or owner aspect, including the autonomy of SOEs to raise funds, bankability, transparency, and disclosure;

(v) **developing green banking capacity** for a responsible banking regulator to provide green credit frameworks, including green credit statistics frameworks (e.g., the Sustainable Banking and Finance Network provides such tools with the support of the International Finance Corporation); and

(vi) **improving green finance (environmental, social, and governance) disclosure** through support to disclosure requirements and disclosure capacity.

The report is consistent with the Asian Development Bank (ADB) goal under Strategy 2030 of supporting SOE reform to help SOEs "access financing on commercial terms and conditions" and in "attracting private investors and bringing in commercial cofinanciers." It builds on previous ADB reports, such as the *Detailed Guidance for Issuing Green Bonds in Developing Countries* and *The Bankable SOE*, both published in 2021.

The report is intended for stakeholders in Asian SOEs, and those facilitating green finance for SOEs.

1 Introduction: Asian State-Owned Enterprises and the Opportunity of Green Finance

Asian State-Owned Enterprises and the Need for a Green Transition

State-owned enterprises (SOEs), including state-linked enterprises, continue to play a major role in both developed and developing countries.[1] SOEs account for 55% of infrastructure investments,[2] 20% of global investment, 5% of employment, and up to 40% of domestic output.[3] They are engaged in many key economic sectors, such as energy, transport, and water. They also provide financial services and jobs to millions of people around the world. Moreover, SOEs provide public services and commercial services and, in many countries, are an important pillar for innovation.

The Dominant Role of State-Owned Enterprises in Emerging Markets

SOEs make up about 60% of total investments in emerging economies, compared to about 9% in developed economies. Particularly in the energy sector—and especially in the fossil fuel sector and networks—SOEs hold a dominant role in emerging economies (Figure 1).

Given their role in basic infrastructure such as energy, SOEs "are responsible for at least 7.49 gigatons of carbon dioxide equivalent annually in direct (Scope 1) emissions[4]... with the true scale of SOE-related emissions likely to be substantially higher.[5] These emissions are equivalent to at least 15% of direct global greenhouse gas (GHG) emissions.[6]

---

[1] Although there is no unique definition of SOEs, it is commonly accepted that they include those companies that are effectively controlled by the state, for example through majority ownership or golden shares, or by decree.

[2] D. Robinett. 2020. Reform State-Owned Enterprises to Avoid a COVID-19 Debt and Investment Crisis. ADB. 3 June.

[3] S. Wong. 2018. The State of Governance at State-Owned Enterprises. Private Sector Opinion. Issue 40. Washington, DC: International Finance Corporation.

[4] Scope 1 emissions include only direct emissions, such as from burning fossil fuels to generate electricity. Scope 1 emissions do not include emissions in the supply chain, such as emissions generated by the purchased electricity, emissions generated downstream by fossil fuels sold by SOEs to other factors, or emissions of portfolio companies.

[5] A. Clark and P. Benoit. 2022. Greenhouse Gas Emissions from State-Owned Enterprises: A Preliminary Inventory. Center on Global Energy Policy. 3 February.

[6] In addition to these Scope 1 emissions, SOEs also play an important role in selling fossil fuels to electricity-producing companies or sourcing products from electricity for their buildings, which have both a climate and a biodiversity impact. Furthermore, many state-owned financial institutions—whether they are development banks or commercial banks—are instrumental in financing economic activities, from fossil fuel companies to green energy.

Figure 1: Investments of State-Owned Enterprises by Economy Type and Sector, 2019

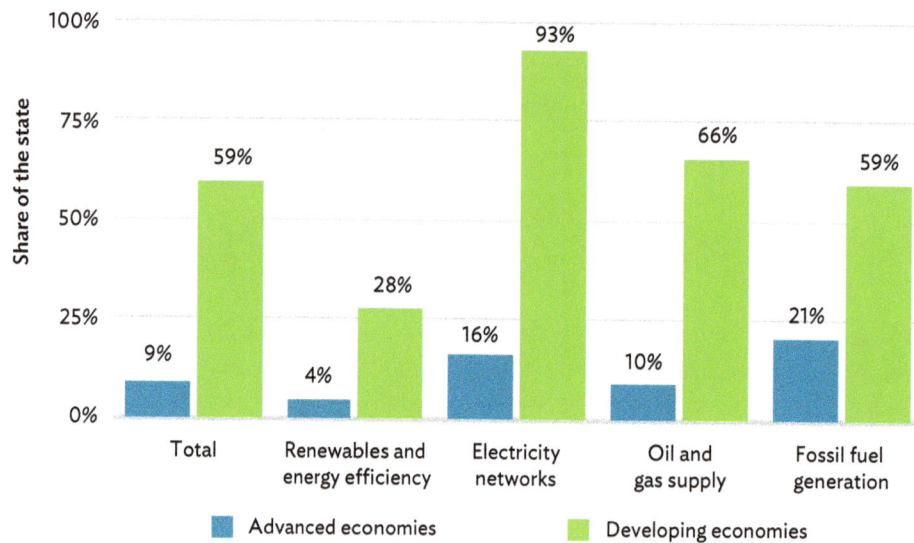

Source: International Energy Agency. Share of State-Owned Energy Investments by Economy Type and Sector, 2019 (accessed 3 May 2022).

According to the ambitions of many Asian countries, these emissions urgently need to be reduced. Most Asian countries have set national climate commitments through nationally determined contributions and policy, with net zero emission or carbon neutrality goals anchored in proposals, policy documents, and laws (Table 1). Half of the Association of Southeast Asian Nations (ASEAN) member states are signatories to the international effort to end coal utilization in the power sector. Brunei Darussalam, Indonesia, the Philippines, Singapore, and Viet Nam signed on to the Global Coal to Clean Power Transition Statement during the 26th United Nations Climate Change Conference (COP26) in 2021.[7] In addition to tackling the climate crisis, leaders from 93 countries and the European Union (EU), including many Asian countries (e.g., Maldives, Mongolia, Nepal, Pakistan, and Sri Lanka), committed in 2020 to reverse biodiversity loss by 2030 through the Leaders Pledge for Nature.[8]

To contribute to the green transition and reduce the risk of global climate change and irreversible biodiversity loss,[9] SOEs need to rapidly reduce GHG emissions and improve environmental performance. In particular, SOEs in the electricity sector, in which SOEs hold a dominating position in many Asian emerging economies, as well as in adjacent sectors with strong SOE footprints, such as transport, water, and financial services, need to accelerate their green transition. SOEs not only have a public responsibility to lead the transition by example, but also have a great opportunity to drive sustainable economic development leading and cooperating with the private sector.

---

[7]   International Renewable Energy Agency (IRENA) and ASEAN Centre for Energy (ACE). 2022. *Renewable Energy Outlook for ASEAN: Towards a Regional Energy Transition* (2nd edition). Abu Dhabi: IRENA / Jakarta: ACE.

[8]   Leaders Pledge for Nature.

[9]   R. E. A. Almond, M. Grooten, and T. Petersen, eds. 2020. *Living Planet Report 2020: Bending the Curve of Biodiversity Loss.* Gland, Switzerland: WWF.

Table 1: Climate Commitments of ADB Developing Member Countries

Country	End Target	End Target Status	Target Year
Afghanistan[a]	Net zero	Proposed/in discussion	2050
Armenia	Other	In policy document	2050
Azerbaijan	Emissions reduction target	In policy document	2030
Bangladesh	Reduction vs. BAU	In policy document	2030
Bhutan	Carbon neutral(ity)	Achieved (self-declared)	2030
Cambodia	Net zero	Achieved (self-declared)	2050
PRC	Carbon neutral(ity)	In policy document	2060
Fiji	Net zero	In law	2050
India	Net zero	Declaration/pledge	2070
Indonesia	Net zero	Proposed/in discussion	2060
Kiribati	Net zero	Proposed/in discussion	2050
Kyrgyzstan	Other	In policy document	2050
Lao PDR	Net zero	In policy document	2050
Malaysia	Carbon neutral(ity)	Declaration/pledge	2050
Marshall Islands	Net zero	In policy document	2050
Micronesia	Net zero	Proposed/in discussion	2050
Myanmar	Net zero	Proposed/in discussion	2050
Nauru	Net zero	Proposed/in discussion	2050
Nepal	Net zero	Proposed/in discussion	2045
Niue	Net zero	Proposed/in discussion	2050
Pakistan	Net zero	Proposed/in discussion	2050
Palau	Net zero	Proposed/in discussion	2050
Papua New Guinea	Net zero	Proposed/in discussion	2050
Philippines	Reduction vs. BAU	In policy document	2030
Solomon Islands	Net zero	Proposed/in discussion	2050
Sri Lanka	Carbon neutral(ity)	In policy document	2060
Thailand	Net zero	Declaration/pledge	2050

continued on next page

Table 1 *continued*

Country	End Target	End Target Status	Target Year
Timor-Leste	Net zero	Proposed/in discussion	2050
Tonga	Net zero	Proposed/in discussion	2050
Turkmenistan	Other	Proposed/in discussion	2030
Tuvalu	Net zero	Proposed/in discussion	2050
Uzbekistan	Emissions intensity target	In policy document	2030
Vanuatu	Net zero	Proposed/in discussion	2050
Viet Nam	Net zero	Declaration/pledge	2050

ADB = Asian Development Bank; BAU = business as usual; Lao PDR = Lao People's Democratic Republic; PRC = People's Republic of China.

[a] ADB placed on hold its assistance in Afghanistan effective 15 August 2021 (ADB. 2021. ADB Statement on Afghanistan. News release. 10 November).

Source: Net Zero Tracker.

Finance for the Green Transition of State-Owned Enterprises

The green transition will require billions. Developing Asia alone will require an estimated $26 trillion just in infrastructure finance during 2016–2030 "to maintain its growth momentum, tackle poverty, and respond to climate change."[10]

With public financing strained, not least to global sovereign debt issues in the wake of the coronavirus disease (COVID-19) pandemic, SOEs must evaluate how to mobilize funds from different sources, including local and global capital markets.[11]

One financial instrument that has gained much attention is green bonds. Important drivers of the success of green bonds have been government and capital market support, the broader interest of investors to reduce environmental risks, and the expansion of government and industry green bond standards.

For example, Asian markets have developed the ASEAN Green Bond Standards through the ASEAN Capital Markets Forum (ACMF).[12] As the ASEAN Green Bond Standards are based on the Green Bond Principles (GBP) of the International Capital Markets Association (ICMA), they are more easily accessible to international investors.

Furthermore, many Asian governments and regulators have issued green finance standards, such as the Green Bond Endorsed Projects Catalogue (2015, updated 2021) in the People's Republic of China (PRC), Indonesia's Green Finance Taxonomy (2022), and Singapore's Green Finance Action Plan (launched in 2019).

---

[10]   Asian Development Bank (ADB). 2017. *Meeting Asia's Infrastructure Needs*. Manila.
[11]   C. Nedopil Wang. 2022. State-Owned Enterprises and Asia's Energy Transition. *East Asia Forum Quarterly*. 14 (2). pp. 19–21.
[12]   The ACMF is a high-level grouping of capital market regulators from all ASEAN jurisdictions. Established in 2004 under the auspices of the ASEAN Finance Ministers, its primary responsibility is to develop a deep, liquid, and integrated regional capital market.

Similarly, many developed countries have published and applied green bond and green finance standards, such as the EU Taxonomy and the market-driven Climate Bonds Taxonomy of the Climate Bonds Initiative (CBI). These standards also affect emerging economies, as most investors interested in green finance are from developed countries and expect international harmonization of green finance standards to lower their research costs and increase the tradability of green bonds. Appendix 1 presents examples of regulatory approaches to green finance standards in the PRC, India, and EU.

An important step toward harmonization of green bond standards relevant for Asian SOEs was the establishment of the International Platform on Sustainable Finance under the leadership of the PRC and the EU. In 2021, the International Platform on Sustainable Finance issued the Common Ground Taxonomy, which allows for a more harmonized categorization of green projects and relevant processes for green bond issuance across jurisdictions, including in emerging economies.

The confluence of interest in green bonds by governments, investors, and issuers helped global green bond markets grow to more than $500 billion in issuances in 2021. Further growth is expected. Global investors are incorporating environmental, social, and governance (ESG) factors when allocating finance and are required to account for portfolio emissions in the EU.

This provides new opportunities to raise green finance from global investors in Asia. At this time, however, most Asian SOEs are trailing in accessing green bond markets.

Opportunities for State-Owned Enterprises through Green Finance

Financing SOEs through capital markets, with a focus on green finance, has five primary advantages for the SOE and its government owner:[13]

(i)   There is **less burden on strained sovereign finance**. Unlike financing of SOEs through government transfers or guarantees (which will directly reduce the government's fiscal space), commercial or nonsovereign borrowing of SOEs adds less direct burden on sovereign debt.

(ii)   The requirement to be "bankable" is an important **catalyst for SOE efficiency and governance**. Accessing capital markets requires SOEs to improve financial sustainability and create acceptable levels of transparency and corporate governance.

(iii) The requirement to be "green" is an important contributor to **improving the corporate strategy** of SOEs, including through a reduction of stranded asset risks and improved ESG performance.

(iv)   Green finance can **lower the financing** for participating companies through a "greemium," where higher government support and investor interest in green finance increase available funding and thus lower financing costs.

(v)   SOEs using green finance can **gain credibility in capital markets** and will be able to raise more financing in the future from both domestic and international investors.[14]

---

13   ADB. 2021. *The Bankable SOE: Commercial Financing for State-Owned Enterprises*. Manila.
14   F. Bancel and D. Glavas. 2017. *The Role of State Ownership as a Determinant of Green Bond Issuance*. Rochester, NY: Social Science Research Network.

The expansion of SOE financing on commercial terms, and in particular through capital markets, would also expand the capacity of supporting industries such as capital markets, local investors, financial institutions, and verifiers that need to work with SOEs to issue bonds, verify green use of proceeds, and trade bonds.[15] This expansion of capital market expertise would also benefit private issuers and can spur further investments in the private sector.[16]

The mobilization of finance, particularly for green projects and activities, through green capital markets (e.g., bonds) and green banking (e.g., green loans) also provides wider benefits for broader economic development:

(i)   Investment in green technologies can support the development of green innovation (e.g., in green energy, transport, and agriculture).

(ii)   Investment in green industries provides additional employment, where green investments tend to generate more additional jobs (e.g., green energy investments provide three times the number of jobs as investment in brown energy).[17]

(iii)   Green energy can lead to a lower cost of doing business through reduced energy costs (Box 1).

Conversely, failing to mobilize green finance to reduce emissions and build a climate-resilient economy risks generating exponentially higher economic, environmental, and social costs—as extreme climate events destroy livelihoods and businesses.[18]

Good State-Owned Enterprise Governance as a Prerequisite for Green Finance

For many SOEs in Asia to access green capital markets, they need to hurdle multiple obstacles to meet the basic requirements of working with international investors:

(i)   Many SOEs need to **improve corporate governance** along a number of axes:

   a. operating at "arm's length" from their government owners to overcome the risk of short-term politically motivated management decisions and foster independent decision-making;

   b. improving transparency of decision-making processes and financial reporting to provide investors with relevant information to evaluate and understand risk; and

   c. improving accountability through better board structures and composition, as well as audits that provide investors with confidence about recourse and influence.

(ii)   SOEs need to **improve their corporate strategy** and develop clear investment strategies that ideally support sustainable development (generating environmental, social, and economic returns), as many investors require a project pipeline to feel confident in investing.

---

[15] U. Volz. 2018. Fostering Green Finance for Sustainable Development in Asia. *ADBI Working Paper Series*. No. 814. Tokyo: Asian Development Bank Institute.

[16] Organisation for Economic Co-operation and Development (OECD). 2018. Energy Sector SOEs: You Have the Power! *OECD on the Level.* 19 April.

[17] H. Engel et al. 2020. Low-Carbon Economic Stimulus after COVID-19. McKinsey Global Institute.

[18] Network for Greening the Financial System. 2019. *A Call for Action: Climate Change as a Source of Financial Risk.* Paris.

Box 1: Investing in Green Energy Brings Tangible Financial Benefits Compared with Fossil Fuels

Many emerging countries have tried to tackle existing power shortages through the construction of fossil fuel power plants, particularly coal-fired power plants. The rationale has been that coal is abundantly available (in many countries, even domestically) and reliable, and the construction and operation costs of coal-fired power plants are "cheap."

However, rapidly falling prices of solar panels and wind turbines have made this assumption outdated. The levelized cost of energy, which measures the total cost of energy from construction to operation and financing, is higher for most fossil fuel-generated electricity than for wind and solar (as presented in the following figure). Increasing costs for fossil fuel financing,[a] the proliferation of domestic carbon prices, risks of carbon border adjustment mechanisms from developed economies, and volatile fossil fuel prices are also important reasons to focus all energy investments on solar and wind energy (including storage to overcome intermittence issues). These have become economically more attractive and provide broader environmental benefits, as well as higher employment compared with fossil fuels.[b]

Figure: Levelized Cost of Energy Comparison–Unsubsidized Analysis

Selected renewable energy generation technologies are cost-competitive with conventional generation technologies under certain circumstances

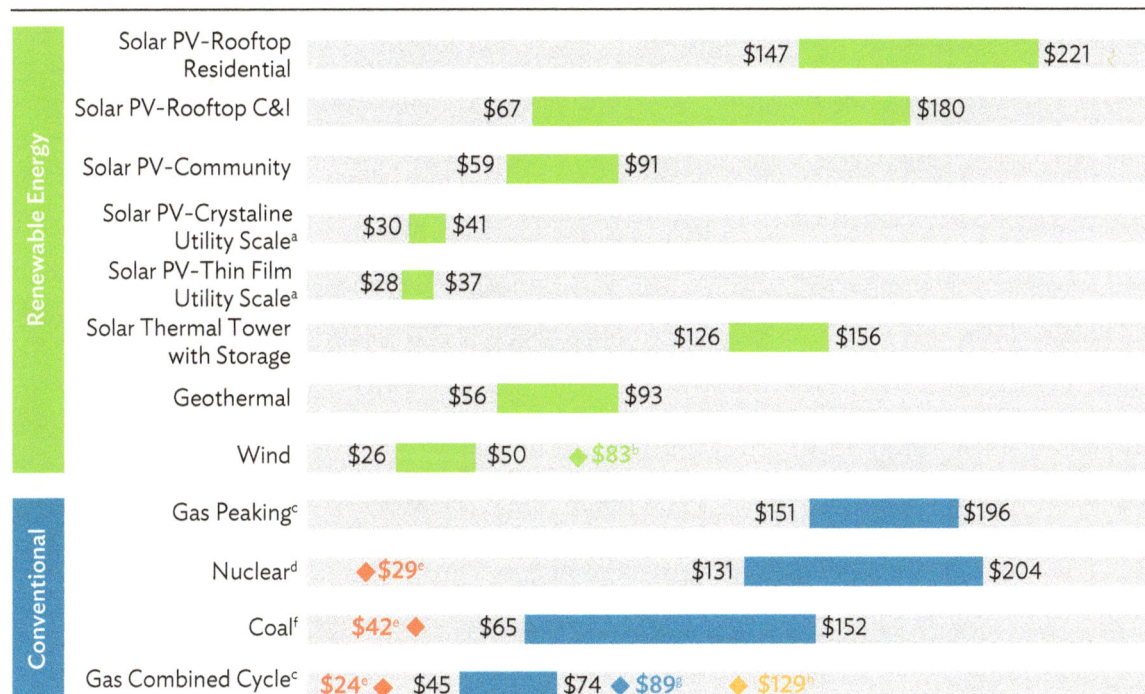

C&I = commercial and industrial, CCGT = combined cycle gas turbine, kg = kilogram, kW = kilowatt, LCOE = levelized cost of energy, MMBtu = metric million British thermal unit , PV = photovoltaic.

Note: Here and throughout this presentation, unless otherwise indicated, the analysis assumes 60% debt at 8% interest rate and 40% equity at 12% cost. Please see page titled "Levelized Cost of Energy Comparison—Sensitivity to Cost of Capital" for cost of capital sensitivities. These results are not intended to represent any particular geography. Please see page titled "Solar PV versus Gas Peaking and Wind versus CCGT—Global Markets" for regional sensitivities to selected technologies.

continued on next page

Box 1 *continued*

^a Unless otherwise indicated herein, the low case represents a single-axis tracking system and the high case represents a fixed-tilt system.

[a]   Unless otherwise indicated herein, the low case represents a single-axis tracking system and the high case represents a fixed-tilt system.

[b]   Represents the estimated implied midpoint of the LCOE of offshore wind, assuming a capital cost range of approximately $2,500—$3.600/kW.

[c]   The fuel cost assumption for Lazard's global, unsubsidized analysis for gas-fired generation resources is $3.45/MMBTU.

[d]   Unless otherwise indicated, the analysis herein does not reflect decommissioning costs, ongoing maintenance-related capital expenditures or the potential economic impacts of federal loan guarantees or other subsidies.

[e]   Represents the midpoint of the marginal cost of operating fully depreciated gas combined cycle, coal and nuclear facilities, inclusive of decommissioning costs for nuclear facilities. Analysis assumes that the salvage value for a decommissioned gas combined cycle or coal asset is equivalent to its decommissioning and site restoration costs. Inputs are derived from a benchmark of operating gas combined cycle, coal and nuclear assets across the United States Capacity factors, fuel, variable and fixed operating expenses are based on upper- and lower-quartile estimates derived from Lazard's research. Please see page titled "Levelized Cost of Energy Comparison—Renewable Energy versus Marginal Cost of Selected Existing Conventional Generation" for additional details.

[f]   High end incorporates 90% carbon capture and storage. Does not include cost of transportation and storage.

[g]   Represents the LCOE of the observed high case gas combined cycle inputs using a 20% blend of "blue" hydrogen, (i.e., hydrogen produced from a steam-methane reformer, using natural gas as a feedstock, and sequestering the resulting carbon dioxide in a nearby saline aquifer). No plant modifications are assumed beyond a 2% adjustment to the plant's heat rate. The corresponding fuel cost is $5.20/MMBtu, assuming $1.39/kg for blue hydrogen.

[h]   Represents the LCOE of the observed high case gas combined cycle inputs using a 20% blend of "green" hydrogen, (i.e., hydrogen produced from an electrolyzer powered by a mix of wind and solar generation and stored in a nearby salt cavern). No plant modifications are assumed beyond a 2% adjustment to the plant's heat rate. The corresponding fuel cost is $10.05/MMBtu, assuming $4.15/kg for green hydrogen.

Source: Lazard estimates.

As a consequence, utilizing green energy provides electricity at a lower cost, while continued investment in fossil-fueled-powered electricity entails higher overall electricity costs. These higher costs would have to be borne either directly by the consumers or indirectly by the taxpayers through the provision of subsidies, making the overall economy less competitive.

[a]   X. Zhou, C. Wilson, and B. Caldecott. 2021. *The Energy Transition and Changing Financing Costs.* Oxford: University of Oxford.
[b]   C. Nedopil Wang. 2022. *Coal Phase-Out in the Belt and Road Initiative (BRI): An Analysis of Chinese-Backed Coal Power from 2014-2020.* Beijing: Green BRI Center, International Institute of Green Finance.

Source: *Lazard.* 2021. Levelized Cost of Energy, Levelized Cost of Storage, and Levelized Cost of Hydrogen. 28 October.

(iii)   SOEs need to **improve bankability with better financial management**, including internal cash flow and external financial risks (e.g., exchange rate risks), as investors need to ensure that the corporate or project cash flow covers the cost of capital.

(iv)   This also means SOEs need to **improve their operational management** to enhance the efficiency of project implementation (e.g., through better human resources and decision-making processes, digitalization) to lower operational costs and ensure desired outcomes on quality, quantity, and timing. This will help reassure investors that their money is efficiently used.

SOEs must also build capacity to actually issue green financial instruments and work with local and international financial and market partners (e.g., investment banks, underwriters, anchor investors, green bond verifiers, and auditors) to fulfill local and international regulatory and voluntary market requirements.

Even if SOEs meet most requirements, investors need to be aware of risks when engaging with them. While SOEs may benefit from explicit or implicit government guarantees that allow them to lower financing costs on capital markets, this may lead to false risk evaluations of SOEs by investors: SOEs can default on loan payments or collapse, as has been witnessed in both developed countries (e.g., the US mortgage firms Freddie Mac and Fannie Mae in 2008) and developing economies (e.g., multiple SOE defaults in the PRC in 2020–2022)[19] with significant losses for investors.

Structure of the Report

SOEs, with their public service mandate and their prominent role in emerging economies, have a key transformative role in the green transition to tackle climate change and biodiversity loss. Acting in cooperation with the private sector, they can take center stage in reducing the risk of catastrophic climate change through emissions reductions, adapting to climate change by building resilience, and reversing the loss of biodiversity.

This report explores how Asian SOEs can benefit from green financial instruments, such as green bonds. First, it analyzes different green finance instruments, and, for their applicability to Asian SOEs. Second, it details the process and requirements for SOEs to issue green financial instruments, such as green bonds. Third, it provides recommendations for support measures from international partners—such as development finance institutions—to accelerate the use of green finance instruments by SOEs.

The report builds on previous Asian Development Bank (ADB) publications, such as the *Detailed Guidance for Issuing Green Bonds in Developing Countries* and *The Bankable SOE*, both published in 2021. It includes resources from the AsianBondsOnline database,[20] the ASEAN Catalytic Green Facility, and related projects. It has been further enriched by interviews with ADB staff and leadership, as well as with external experts.

Apart from relying on public finance through government subsidies and transfers, SOEs can utilize commercial finance through green debt and equity instruments. Under the right circumstances, SOEs can also access public capital markets, for example by issuing green bonds.

---

[19]   S. Shen, A. Galbraith, and T. Westbrook. 2020. Bond Defaults Show Beijing's War on Debt Is Back. *Reuters*. 25 November.
[20]   Asian Bonds Online.

2 Green Finance for the Green Transition of State-Owned Enterprises

Growing Toolbox of Green Finance Instruments

Traditionally, most Asian financial systems that provided finance for SOEs are dominated by banking, where companies relied on credits and loans (in addition to SOEs receiving direct funding through government budgets). Yet, given the wide recognition of the need to mobilize more finance and the interest to develop local capital markets, SOEs can utilize a growing toolbox of green finance instruments that also include mobilizing finance from local capital markets by issuing, for example, Sustainable Development Goal (SDG), green, blue, or transition bonds. The relationship between these aspects is shown in the sustainable finance landscape (Figure 2). For example, within green finance, several subsectors can be addressed, including GHG emissions, climate resilience, biodiversity outcomes, or water-related issues (through blue finance).

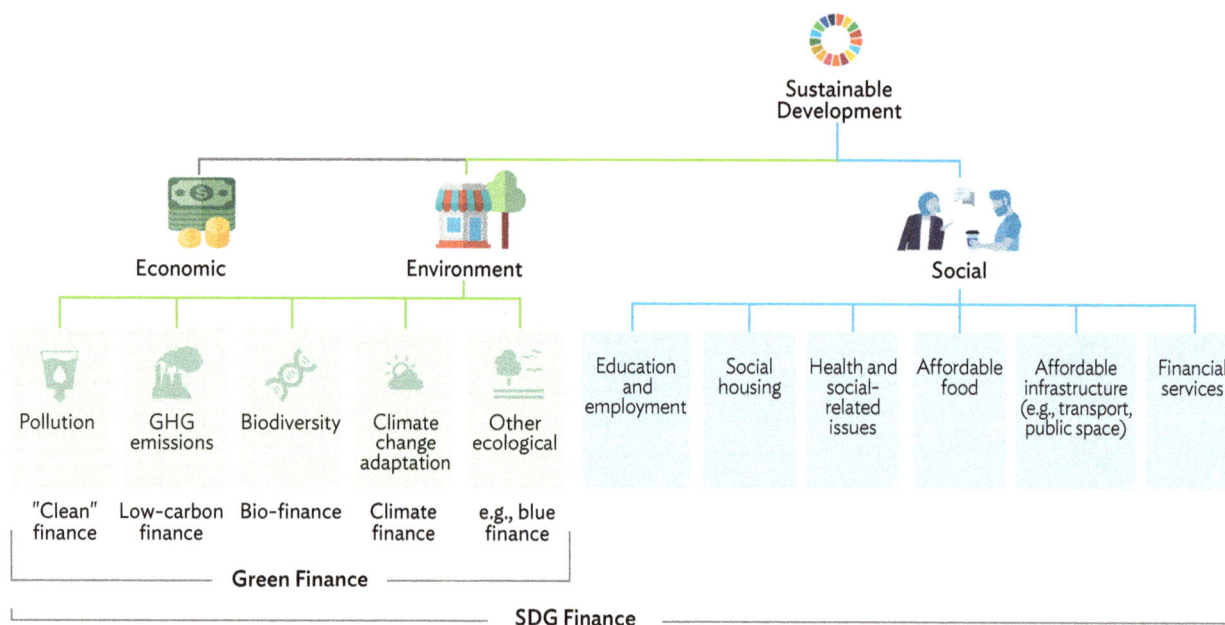

Figure 2: Sustainable Finance Landscape

GHG = greenhouse gas, SDG = Sustainable Development Goal.

Source: C. Nedopil Wang and Q. Xu. 2020. *Technical Report on SDG Finance Taxonomy (China)*. Beijing: United Nations Development Programme.

Figure 3: Sustainable Finance Instrument Toolbox

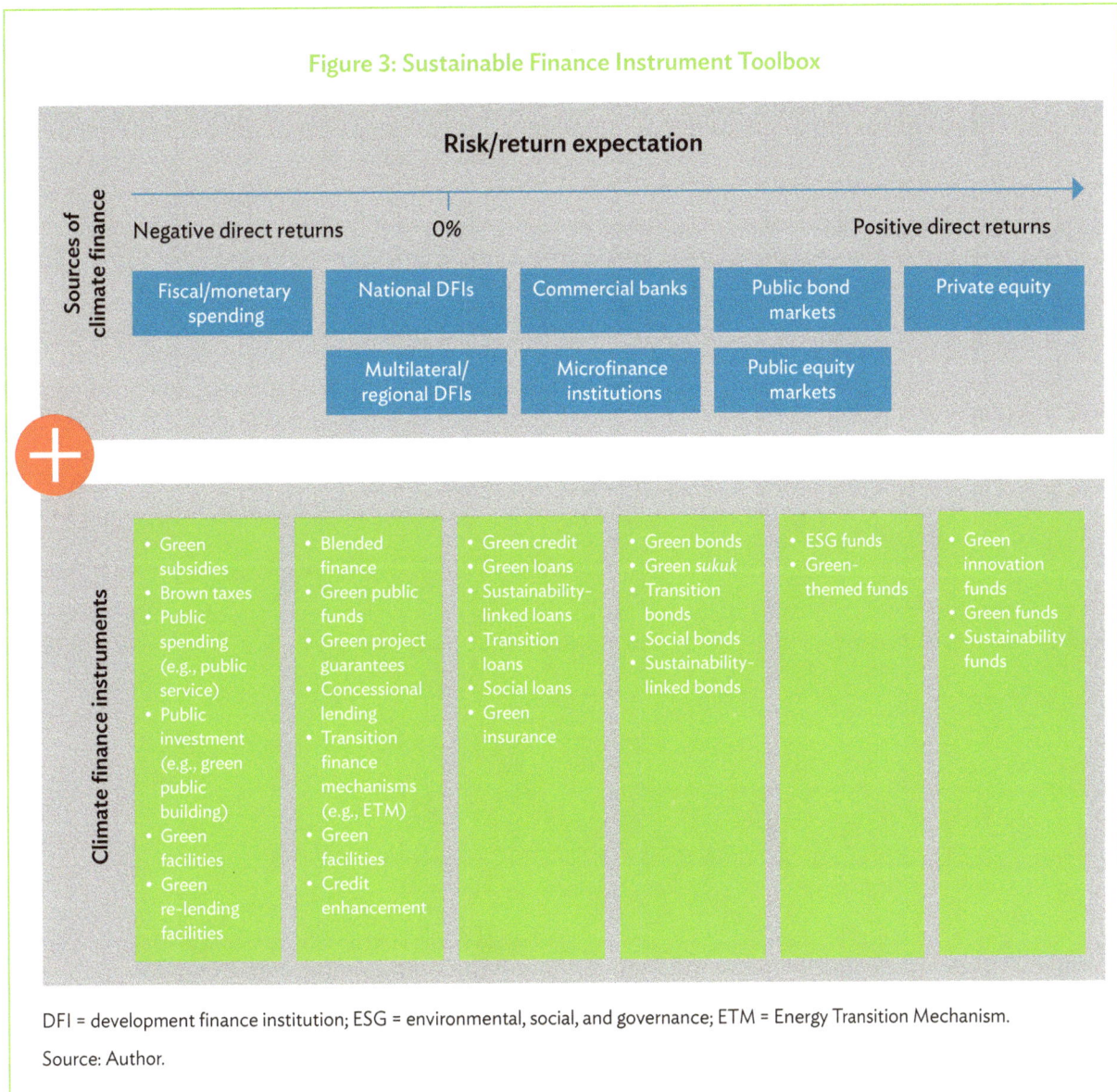

Risk/return expectation

Negative direct returns   0%   Positive direct returns

Sources of climate finance				
Fiscal/monetary spending	National DFIs	Commercial banks	Public bond markets	Private equity
	Multilateral/ regional DFIs	Microfinance institutions	Public equity markets	

Climate finance instruments

• Green subsidies • Brown taxes • Public spending (e.g., public service) • Public investment (e.g., green public building) • Green facilities • Green re-lending facilities	• Blended finance • Green public funds • Green project guarantees • Concessional lending • Transition finance mechanisms (e.g., ETM) • Green facilities • Credit enhancement	• Green credit • Green loans • Sustainability-linked loans • Transition loans • Social loans • Green insurance	• Green bonds • Green *sukuk* • Transition bonds • Social bonds • Sustainability-linked bonds	• ESG funds • Green-themed funds	• Green innovation funds • Green funds • Sustainability funds

DFI = development finance institution; ESG = environmental, social, and governance; ETM = Energy Transition Mechanism.

Source: Author.

For each of the green development goals, various financial instruments can be utilized. The specific structure of the financial instrument depends on the risk and return profile of the underlying asset (e.g., the SOE itself or the project that the SOE wants to finance), and the investor type. Figure 3 shows how, for example, fiscal and monetary spending from governments often has a very low (possibly even zero or negative) return expectation and provides public investment for SOEs or public infrastructure. At the other end of the spectrum are private equity funds, accepting high risks in exchange for the expectation of high returns, which can provide financing (often equity or possibly mezzanine capital) through green innovation funds. In between are public bond and public equity markets, with lower risk-taking and return expectations. These investors invest in green bonds, green *sukuk* (fixed income instruments), ESG funds, and green equity.

Besides green bonds (described in more detail below), these other commercial green and sustainable finance instruments are receiving increasing attention:

(i) **Green loans,** which provide bank financing through loans to business operations. The selection criteria for eligible projects may be similar to those for green bonds, but reporting requirements and covenants are dependent on the arrangement with the commercial bank. The bank itself may utilize green bonds to mobilize funds for green loans, particularly if the underlying loans meet relevant green finance criteria.

(ii) **Transition loans and bonds**, which provide financing for companies (and, to a lesser extent, projects) that do not fulfill the requirements for green finance but build on the promise and strategy to transition from business models with significant environmental harm to less harmful business models.

(iii) **Social bonds** (an example is presented in Box 2) raise capital from capital markets to invest in social projects, with a focus on social groups that are otherwise at risk of being left behind. The United Nations Development Programme issued an SDG Finance Taxonomy in 2020, focusing on social projects, which provides a catalog of projects in six categories (Figure 2) and relevant impact indicators.[21]

(iv) **Sustainability-linked loans and bonds**, which link the cost of the loan to the ESG performance of the issuer or project. This requires a clear understanding of the financing's desired positive impact, with sound and clear measurement, reporting, and validation—as the cost of the instrument depends on the actual performance of the company or project.

An important factor for green finance instruments is that they require positive financial returns for investors— with the exception of government funding or, partly, development finance funding.

Box 2: Social Bonds for Thailand

In June 2022, the Government Savings Bank (GSB) of Thailand became the first state-owned financial institution to issue a social bond under the ASEAN Social Bond Standards.[a]

According to the bond catalog, the GSB plans to use the B10 billion ($295 million) bond's proceeds in its ambition to reduce inequality and eradicate extreme poverty. Specific social projects supported, for example by low-interest loans to customers, include
- improving living conditions;
- reducing informal debt;
- developing occupational capabilities capabilities, e.g., for the unemployed and vulnerable groups; and
- supporting entrepreneurs as well as small and medium-sized businesses.

The Asian Development Bank supported the GSB in the issuance of the bond, which was sold to Thai institutional investors and high-net-worth individuals.

Apart from the mobilization of finance through the bond, the issuance of the bond also contributed to the development of the Thai sustainable bond market.

---

[a] ASEAN Capital Markets Forum (ACMF). 2018. ASEAN Social Bond Standards. Phnom Penh.

Source: Asian Development Bank. 2022. ADB Supports Thailand's First Social Bond Issued by State-Owned Government Savings Bank. News release. 29 June.

---

[21] C. Nedopil Wang and Q. Xu. 2020. *Technical Report on SDG Finance Taxonomy (China)*. Beijing: United Nations Development Programme.

Green Bonds

Defining Green Bonds

Green bonds, one of the fastest-growing asset classes for sustainable finance with strong relevance for SOEs, are financial instruments that tie the proceeds of a bond issue to green investments. International Capital Markets Association (ICMA) Green Bond Principles (GBP), for example, define green bonds as "any type of bond instruments where the proceeds will be exclusively applied to finance or refinance in part or in full new and/or existing eligible green projects."[22]

Types of Green Bonds

Green bonds (and similarly other SDG-related bonds) can be divided into different types of bonds, ranging from "use of proceeds" bonds—which earmark proceeds for new green projects—to project bonds and green *sukuk* (Table 2). Certified green bonds, loans, and sukuk (and other debt instruments such as green deposits, leases, commercial paper, and repos), for example, have been issued by over 220 issuers from 40 economies (as of January 2022).[23]

Table 2: Types of Green Bonds

Type	Proceeds Raised by Bond Sale	Debt Recourse
"Use of proceeds" bond	Earmarked for green projects	Recourse to the issuer: the same credit rating applies as to the issuer's other bonds.
"Use of proceeds" revenue bond or ABS bond	Earmarked for or to refinance green projects	Revenue streams from the issuers through fees, taxes, etc. are collateral for the debt.
Project bond	Ringfenced for the specific underlying green project(s)	Recourse is only to the project's assets and balance sheet.
Securitization (ABS) bond	To refinance portfolios of green projects or earmarked for green projects	Recourse is to a group of projects that have been grouped together (e.g., solar leases or green mortgages).
Covered bond	Earmarked for eligible projects included in the covered pool	Recourse is to the issuer and, if the issuer is unable to repay the bond, to the covered pool.
Other debt instruments	Earmarked for eligible projects	

ABS = asset-backed security.

Source: Climate Bonds Initiative. Explaining Green Bonds.

---

22   ICMA. 2021. Green Bond Principles: Voluntary Process Guidelines for Issuing Green Bonds. Paris.

23   *Climate Bonds Initiative* (CBI). 2022. Certified Green Issuance Passes $200bn – Expansion of Climate Bonds Standard in 2022: Basic Chemicals, Cement, Steel in Pipeline. 11 January.

Green Bond Standards

Various standards for green bonds have been developed that could be relevant for Asian SOEs depending on the jurisdiction. The standards describe the process and requirements of green bond issuance and provide definitions for investors and issuers on how to raise, use, describe, and report on green bonds.

A challenge for SOEs is to select the right standard, as the "market for green bond standards," with requirements that are not fully aligned, can be confusing. For example, in some jurisdictions (e.g., EU, Indonesia, PRC), regulators are increasingly active in defining the standards. For other international issuances, private organization standards, such as the ICMA GBP or the Climate Bond Taxonomy of the Climate Bonds Initiative (CBI), are more appropriate.

The differences between the standards may relate to, for example, the type of eligible projects (e.g., in the PRC's Green Bond Endorsed Projects Catalogue, some projects related to coal are allowed, contrary to CBI standards); the use of proceeds requirement (e.g., in the PRC, only 50% of the bond proceeds needs to be earmarked for green activities); or in the reporting requirements. Another distinction is in their scope of application, with standards issued by regulators or government institutions usually applicable only for domestic issuances (e.g., relevant for tax or government support reasons); while nongovernment standards (e.g., CBI) can be more broadly applied—and more easily understood by global investors without the need to study each jurisdiction's own requirements for defining green bonds.

For SOEs in Asia, various standards can be applicable, and often the choice of the standard depends on the investors the SOE wants to attract, and the market in which the SOE wants to issue its bond. It is also possible to verify the green bond issuance using several standards. For example, numerous Chinese SOEs have issued green bonds domestically, using the domestic green bond taxonomy as a standard; they have also issued green bonds in domestic and international markets using the CBI standard to attract more international investors. From an investor's perspective, international standards are often preferable, as these are more familiar. Using international standards also allows bonds to trade more easily among investors on secondary markets.

Appendix 2 provides a comparison of green bond standards that are relevant for Asian SOEs. It analyzes green bond standards issued by regulators (e.g., EU, Singapore, PRC) and standard-setters (e.g., CBI, ASEAN) for their different applications and core components.

Green Bond Market Developments

The green bond market has been growing rapidly over the past 8 years across multiple jurisdictions. The CBI data show that total annual green bond issuance globally increased from $37 billion in 2014 to $522 billion in 2021 (Figure 4).[24] In 2021, developed countries accounted for 75% and emerging markets 21% (up from 10% in 2020) of global issuances. Asia and the Pacific region accounted for about 25% of global green bond issuances in 2021. However, despite their central role for development in the region, government-backed entities in developing Asia and the Pacific countries accounted for only 13% of the green bond market between 2014 and 2021 (compared with, e.g., 15% in Europe). This leaves much room for growth.

---

[24]   CBI. Interactive Data Platform (accessed 18 May 2022).

Figure 4: Green Bond Issuances 2014–2021 for Different Regions *(top)* and Cumulative Share of Green Bond Issuance for Different Issuers in Developing Countries in Asia and the Pacific *(bottom)*

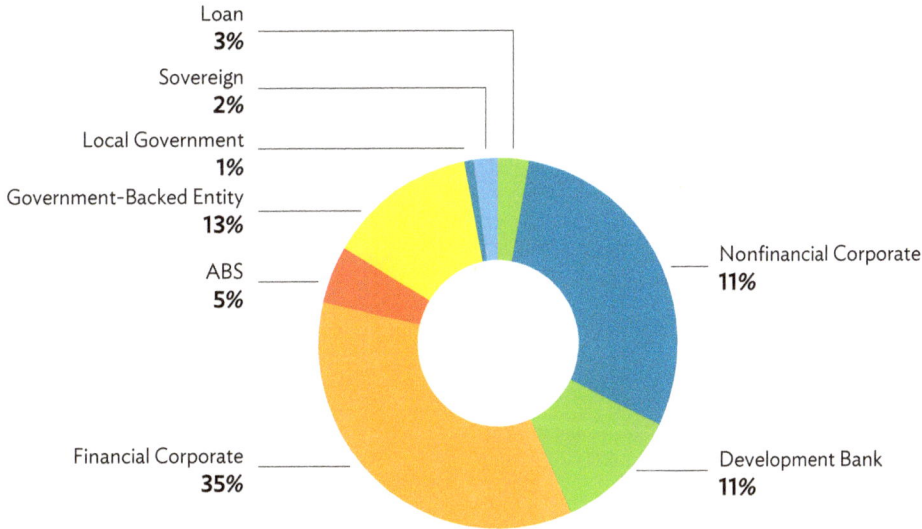

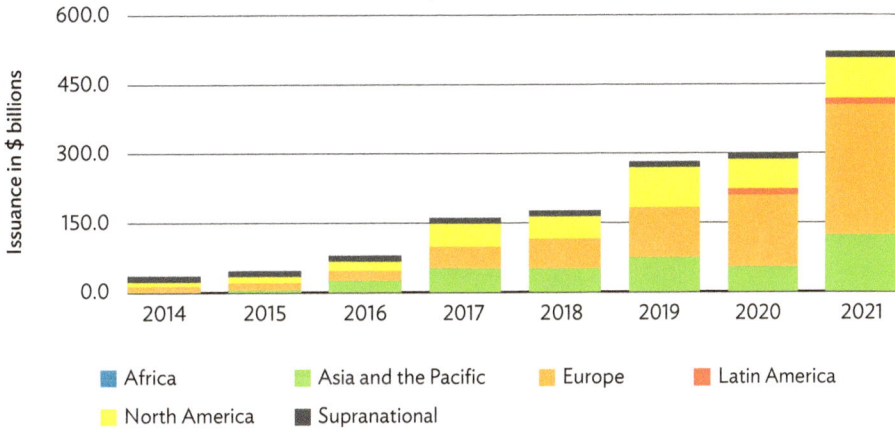

ABS = asset-backed security.
Source: Author using the Climate Bonds Initiative data.

State-Owned Enterprise Benefits from Green Bond Issuances

Green bond issuances can play an important role in mobilizing finance from a variety of investors for green projects and for refinancing SOEs. While green bond issuance often requires more preparation and reporting compared with regular bonds, it has several advantages for SOEs, particularly if the bond is independently verified:

(i)   A green bond issuance **can attract more investors**. This has two main reasons: (a) investors perceive a lower risk in the bond because of the relatively high transparency requirements of the issuer, and (b) more investors are interested in green finance because of investors' desires and requirements to reduce environmental risks in their portfolios.

(ii)   More investor interest can lead to a situation where the **financing cost may be lower through a "greemium"** of green bonds. However, not every green bond will be cheaper than a regular bond.

(iii) Green bond issuances provide the SOE with an incentive to **improve corporate governance and public reporting** because of capital market requirements on disclosure, risk management, and accountability.

(iv)   Green bond issuances provide the SOE with an incentive to **improve its corporate strategy**, as green bond issuances often focus on a new green project that needs to be bankable, and therefore environmental and social sustainability are becoming strategic areas for finance and strategy departments.

(v)   By utilizing the proceeds of green bonds, the SOE not only provides a contribution to the green transition but also **reduces the risk of "stranded assets,"**[25] with fewer of the SOE's assets being unaligned with the green transition.

Local Capital Market Benefits of State-Owned Enterprise Green Bond Issuances

To issue green bonds, SOEs need green bond markets. Green bond markets can be successful only if they can bring together green bond issuers and investors in sufficient scale and frequency to provide liquidity in the market. This requires sufficient numbers and high volumes of lower-risk green bonds, as well as sufficient trading of green bonds for investors to be able to sell and buy bonds depending on their liquidity and risk preferences.

However, green bond markets in many Asian developing countries continue to be underdeveloped, with few or no green bond issuances. Reasons for this underdevelopment vary, and include factors such as lack of applicable sustainable finance standards, nontransparent information and poor quality data, small capital base without liquidity, small pipeline of issuances, and limited capacity of market players or supporting capacity (e.g., of green bond verifiers).[26]

While SOEs can utilize international green bond markets to issue green bonds, SOEs that issue green bonds locally can be an important driver for local green bond market development. Indeed, over the past decades, green bond market development has often been driven by green bond issuances from policy and development banks, as well as by sovereign and sovereign-backed issuers that utilize their relatively better risk ratings to attract investors. For example, in 2007, the European Investment Bank issued the world's first climate-related "climate

---

[25]   "Stranded assets" refer to assets that become unproductive because of climate change. They can include real estate that is becoming flooded, agriculture that is unproductive because of lack of water, hydropower plants that cannot operate for lack of water, and high-emitting assets (e.g., coal plants) that have to close down as a result of cheaper alternatives or increased cost of operations (e.g., because of domestic or international carbon prices). These assets have to be written off the balance sheets with significant financial risks.

[26]   ACMF. 2020. Roadmap for ASEAN Sustainable Capital Markets. Phnom Penh.

awareness bond," which played a fundamental role in the development of green bond markets.[27] The first Asian green bond was issued in 2013 by Export-Import Bank of Korea, raising $500 million.[28] Indonesia saw its first green bond launch in April 2014 by PT Ciputra Residence, a residential property developer, with a partial credit guarantee from the International Finance Corporation worth Rp500 billion ($44 million). In July 2014, Advanced Semiconductor Engineering from Taipei,China issued the first Asian corporate green bond without public support.[29] In the People's Republic of China, about 97% of green bond issuances between 2016 and March 2022 were by government and SOE issuers. By 2020, ADB had raised over $10 billion, since its first green bond issuance of $500 million in March 2015.[30]

Government-backed entities, such as SOEs, have been an important driver of green bond market development for various reasons:

(i)   the lower risks of green bonds issued by government-backed entities such as SOEs, compared with their commercial counterparts, mostly because of the implicit or explicit government guarantee;

(ii)   the volume of SOE green bond issuance being greater than many private companies' issuance because of the size of the SOE and/or the underlying asset (e.g., larger infrastructure projects)—and this larger volume of green bonds improving the overall liquidity of the market;

(iii) diversification of risk, because different SOEs—as well as state-owned financial institutions issuing green bonds for diverse projects, and the use of proceeds market—create different bond risk profiles and maturities;

(iv)   green bond benchmark rates being set through green SOE bonds relevant for other issuers; and

(v)   the building of local technical capacity through the regular issuance and trading of green financial bonds for markets, issuers, traders, and supporting service organizations (e.g., underwriters and verifiers).

In consequence, SOE-driven green bond issuances can catalyze system-level change, creating a blueprint for other issuers. They also offer investors a relatively low-risk and large investment opportunity, which is particularly interesting for international investors. SOE green bond issuances have a signaling power, supporting local capital market development relevant for mobilizing private sector capital, with the potential to unlock broader green bond issuances in the market.

Applicability of Green Finance Instruments for State-Owned Enterprises

While green financial instruments have multiple benefits, not all SOEs are in an equal position to use these different instruments. Table 3 highlights how various green finance instruments have different requirements for the SOE, depending on its agency in relation to its government owner, profit motivation and financial leverage, capacity (e.g., for risk management), operational efficiency, transparency, and "greenness." For example, green government funds have lower requirements compared with ESG funds and green bonds, which are both driven by commercial investor requirements. Specifically, green government funds likely require lower agency by the SOE to deal with capital markets; they also require less capacity for financial management. Transition bonds, meanwhile, require high capacity and agency, but less greenness from the SOE.

---

[27]   European Investment Bank. 2021. *Key Findings – Evaluation of the EIB's Climate Awareness Bonds*. Luxembourg.

[28]   J. Darcy and T. Kelly. 2015. *Green Bonds: Emergence of the Australian and Asian Markets.* Melbourne: Allens / Hong Kong, China: Linklaters.

[29]   V. Münzer-Jones and D. Johnson. 2016. *Recent Developments in the Asian Green Bond Markets.* Norton Rose Fulbright.

[30]   ADB. 2021. *ADB Green Bond Newsletter and Impact Report.* Manila.

An SOE hoping to utilize the green finance toolbox should therefore evaluate which requirements it can meet, and which financial instrument is most applicable. As green bonds have great potential to raise significant amounts of capital, the following section highlights the requirements and process for issuing green bonds for SOEs.

Table 3: Overview of Requirements for Utilizing Green Finance Instruments

Type	Agency	Profit Motivation, including Financial Leverage	Capacity (e.g., Risk Management, Financial Ability)	Operational Efficiency (Exposure to Market)	Transparency	Green Eligibility
Green government funds	Medium	Medium	Medium	Low	Medium	Low–high
Blended finance	Medium	Medium	Medium	Medium	Medium–high	Medium
Transition bonds	High	High	High	Medium	High	Medium
Green credit	Medium	Medium	Medium	Medium	Medium	High
Green bonds	High	High	High	High	High	High
ESG funds	High	High	High	High	High	High

ESG = environmental, social, and governance.

Source: Author.

3 How to Issue Green State-Owned Enterprise Bonds

SOEs wanting to issue green financial instruments, such as green bonds, need to fulfill two main prerequisites: the SOE and its green asset (e.g., project or company) must be (i) bankable and (ii) green, by following applicable domestic or internationally recognized processes and standards for issuing green bonds.

The challenges to overcome can be summarized as follows:

(i) **Enabling environment**. Is the SOE permitted to raise capital on the capital market?

(ii) **Governance issues**
   a. **Governance**. Is SOE governance (ownership, strategy, etc.) appropriate?
   b. **Risk management**. Does the SOE have sufficient risk management capacity?
   c. **Transparency**. Can the SOE measure, verify, and report on green bond performance?
   d. **Credibility**. Is the SOE credible on green strategy and implementation?
   e. **Management capacity**. Does the SOE have the management capacity to issue and manage green bonds?

(iii) **Green finance issuances**
   a. **Bankability**. Is the SOE or the relevant project financially bankable?
   b. **Green eligibility**. Does the SOE have eligible green projects?

Securing the Enabling Environment to Issue State-Owned Enterprise Green Bonds

A prerequisite in SOE governance to issue sustainable financial instruments such as green bonds is the enabling environment that permits SOEs to raise capital from nongovernment sources. Usually, SOEs that are partly listed on stock exchanges have more autonomy to raise funds from capital markets through existing nongovernment investors in the company. For fully state-owned entities, the ability to raise funds from capital markets depends on the SOE's arrangement with the owner (e.g., a dedicated government ownership entity, such as Khazanah Nasional Berhad in Malaysia, or the government itself through specific line ministries or the Ministry of Finance).

SOEs that depend on their government owner to provide finance need to obtain permission to raise funds on capital markets and to build the technical capacity to engage with capital markets. Permission to engage with capital markets may have to be provided for the SOE treasury (i.e., how far can the SOE independently manage its finance) and/or for the SOE management team (i.e., do SOE managers have the autonomy or permission to raise funds and disclose relevant information).

The more experience and capacity an SOE has gained in engaging with capital markets and private investors, the easier the green bond or green financial instrument placement will be. Conversely, an SOE without any capacity or experience may not even have a relevant credit rating.

To overcome the capacity gap, in several countries, for example Japan, ministries have established centers to support the issuance of green bonds for private companies. Countries with less experienced SOEs could establish similar centers to support SOEs in issuing their green bonds, within the relevant ministry or SOE holding entity. Further capacity building can be supported through technical assistance projects, and by seconding staff and managers from more experienced to less experienced SOEs.

Improving State-Owned Enterprise Corporate Governance

Engaging with capital markets requires a certain level of transparency and accountability of the SOE toward investors. Investors typically value SOEs more highly if they have better, consistent public reporting with transparent processes and can be held accountable for misconduct. Conversely, companies and SOEs that are opaque—providing little opportunity for investors to engage, and low access to efficient redress in case of breach of contract—are less attractive to investors.

For many Asian SOEs, addressing governance issues has been a core challenge. Across Asia, some SOEs have successfully improved corporate governance and issued bonds and listed parts of their shares on capital markets. However, the majority of SOEs in Asia have little experience in capital markets; they often also lack sufficient incentive, capacity, and authority to reform governance to meet investor standards.

However, for SOEs interested in issuing sustainable and green finance instruments such as green bonds, ensuring good governance is crucial.

Addressing SOE governance covers several key aspects, depending on the relationship between its owners (e.g., fully or partially state-owned), the SOE's internal systems and controls of management (e.g., the board's role), risk identification and management (including ESG risks), the strategy-setting process (including the selection of projects), and reporting and disclosure.

Many resources have been developed to address SOE governance:
   (i)   the *Organisation for Economic Co-operation and Development (OECD) Guidelines on Corporate Governance of State-Owned Enterprises*, 2015 Edition;[31]
   (ii)   ADB's *Guidance Note on State-Owned Enterprise Reform in Sovereign Projects and Programs*, 2021;[32]
   (iii) ADB's *The Bankable SOE: Commercial Financing for State-Owned Enterprises*, 2021 (footnote 13); and
   (iv)   World Bank's *Corporate Governance of State-Owned Enterprises: A Toolkit*, 2014.[33]

In addition to these standards, when considering investing in SOEs, it is relevant for green investors to look at whether there is a clear green strategy developed by the board and top management that is directly related to the company's capacities for implementation and investment strategy. This could mean, for example, a credible green investment (or brown divestment) program based on a publicly stated environmental strategy. A green development strategy defines the medium- to long-term ambitions, projects, business models, and revenue streams of the company that require green finance (which can be raised through green bonds, as well as through other channels). A credible green development strategy signals sincerity, foresight, and top-level support within the company to advance its green transition. Without such a strategy, a green bond issuance could be defined as

---

[31]   OECD. 2015. *OECD Guidelines on Corporate Governance of State-Owned Enterprises*. 2015 Edition. Paris.
[32]   ADB. 2021. *Guidance Note on State-Owned Enterprise Reform in Sovereign Projects and Programs*. Manila.
[33]   World Bank. 2014. *Corporate Governance of State-Owned Enterprises: A Toolkit*. Washington, DC.

a pilot green bond, while it could make it more difficult to attract private and particularly institutional investors as they fear reputational risks. For example, a coal company that issues a one-off bond for a green project, but otherwise continues to fund coal-related projects, may be unattractive for green investors because of both reputational and economic risks (i.e., as the coal company may run into stranded asset risks on a corporate level). The green transformation strategy should ideally be communicated clearly with the markets. This strategy needs to be clearly publicized by the board with strong support and endorsement by the (government) owners.

Timely, accurate, and regular reporting on the use of proceeds—and potentially the impact of sustainability-linked instruments—is required, particularly for green financial instruments. SOEs interested in issuing green financial instruments should therefore ensure they have sufficient capacity and autonomy in providing this timely information to investors and, ideally, the public. They should preferably also have the ability to hire independent verifiers and auditors to ensure the credibility of such reports.

More broadly, green and sustainable investors may have an even stronger interest than regular investors in sound overall SOE governance. This would include strong stakeholder engagement, a credible fight against corruption, merit-based employment policies, and a board with the necessary authority, competence, integrity, and accountability. Good SOE governance can be based, for example, on the *OECD Guidelines on Corporate Governance for State-Owned Enterprises* (footnote 31).

Ensuring Bankable and "Green" Issuances

Once an SOE meets basic governance requirements, it must ensure the green bond issuance meets bankability requirements (i.e., generating sufficient revenues to service the bond) and that the bond's greenness can be guaranteed.

Improving Bankability

Investors expect the bond issuer to be able to pay the interest and principal of the bond. This requires the issuer or the underlying asset of the bond to be "bankable" based on current and projected cash flows, , and the internal (company) and external risks affecting those cash flows (Figure 5). Investors will be keen to see that the SOE bond's risk and return profile is as good or better than that provided by alternative issuers. This requires the SOE to manage its external and internal risk factors.

External risk factors, such as government, investor, and economic risks, can impact the bankability of an SOE green bond and possibly lead to requirements for higher interest rates to compensate. Many external factors cannot be controlled by the SOE, but must be monitored and managed properly (e.g., exchange rate reserves or hedging to reduce foreign exchange risks).

Internal risks affecting bankability, conversely, can be directly controlled and reduced by the SOE. Besides governance improvements, business decisions and operational processes contribute to financial risks and need to be addressed. These include improvements in operational efficiency to ensure timely and high-quality delivery of projects, services, and goods that are the basis of cash flows. Operational processes, which many Asian SOEs can and must improve, include human resources to attract and retain talent, operational decision-making to reduce friction and increase speed, and manufacturing and delivery efficiencies (e.g., through digitalization).

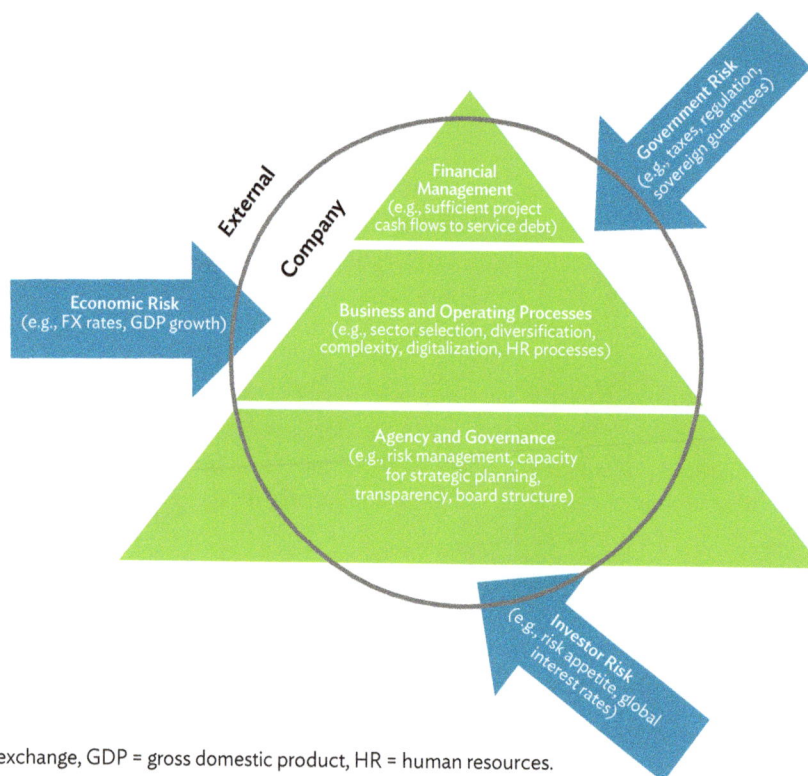

Figure 5: Bankability Factors for State-Owned Enterprise Corporate Debt

Financial Management (e.g., sufficient project cash flows to service debt)

Business and Operating Processes (e.g., sector selection, diversification, complexity, digitalization, HR processes)

Agency and Governance (e.g., risk management, capacity for strategic planning, transparency, board structure)

Government Risk (e.g., taxes, regulation, sovereign guarantees)

Economic Risk (e.g., FX rates, GDP growth)

Investor Risk (e.g., risk appetite, global interest rates)

External / Company

FX = foreign exchange, GDP = gross domestic product, HR = human resources.

Source: Author, based on Asian Development Bank. 2021. *The Bankable SOE: Commercial Financing for State-Owned Enterprises*. Manila.

A further prerequisite for SOEs to improve bankability and help investors understand potential risks is **good financial management**, for example through better cash flow planning. A further tool for investors to evaluate a company's performance and its bankability entails independently audited balance sheets and timely annual reports, which SOEs should produce accordingly.

A viable option to improve the bankability of many SOEs and their projects (depending on regulation and the SOE capacity) and overcome SOE-specific governance and management risks (and possibly ensure a focus on green assets) is to **establish a special business unit outside the SOE** that issues and utilizes the green bond. This unit can take the form of a newly formed subsidiary (e.g., a green energy subsidiary), a joint venture (JV) with another public or private entity, or a special-purpose vehicle in a public–private partnership (PPP). Such models are prevalent in many infrastructure projects (e.g., roads and energy projects) that involve both public actors and private partners. PPPs take a wide range of organizational forms, depending on the local circumstances, laws, the project, and the experience of the actors (Figure 6)—ranging from fully publicly owned entities with private contractors to mostly privately owned JVs with SOE participation.

The special business unit formed will be incorporated and will be responsible for taking all the steps necessary for a green bond issuance (e.g., green bond framework, reporting, validation, etc.). Ideally, the unit will have more flexibility to hire relevant staff and external experts and set up appropriate governance systems.

Box 3: Improving State-Owned Enterprise Efficiency
—The Case of the Phnom Penh Water Supply Authority

In 2004, the Phnom Penh Water Supply Authority (PPWSA), the state-owned water supply company in Phnom Penh, Cambodia, was awarded the Water Prize of the Asian Development Bank (ADB). This award is conferred on exemplary project agencies that have established sound practices in implementing ADB's Water for All Policy. In 2006, the World Bank wrote that the PPWSA was "unlike a typical water utility in Asia," owing to its massive improvements in water service delivery and commercial performance.

But things had not always been like this. Ek Sonn Chan, who was appointed general director of the PPWSA in 1993, remembered that the PPWSA used to be *the perfect bad example. You could have had a water pipe running in front of your house and still not be able to have a connection.*

When Chan took office in 1993, services reached only 20% of Phnom Penh's citizens and provided a mere 77 liters of water per person during 10 hours of service per day. This is well below the service delivery 20 years earlier. Even worse, much of the water was not potable, with the consequence that almost a third of all hospitalizations were linked to water-related diseases. Also, there was no money to spend, as lack of staff discipline and lack of systems to control water supply left 72% of supplied water unaccounted for and did not generate revenues. This led to about KR809 million ($490,000) in losses per year.

The success of the PPWSA was built on governance and operational improvements in various aspects, driven by ADB's support and facilitated by three interrelated improvements:

Service quality
(i) A regulated model for water supply enabled urban poor people to pay less for reliable and potable piped water supply than to an illegal network of resellers. This improved health outcomes and service provision, as well as increased revenue.
(ii) Long-term community engagement was important, for example to ensure continuous billing and a reduction in illegal water usage.
(iii) Continuous investments in infrastructure and delivery were crucial—enabled by external financing—and helped improve service delivery.

Organizational culture
(i) Appointment of a capable, determined, and reliable leader with strong communication skills helped build trust in the SOE.
(ii) A stable, strongly committed general director and management team ensured long-term improvement, not just a "sprint."
(iii) Cost recovery was vital: the tariff structure allowed the recovery of all operational costs; however, this needed to be supported by operational efficiency.
(iv) The autonomy of the PPWSA was essential to financial and operational sustainability, for example by improving staff recruitment and salary structures. This allowed the PPWSA to eradicate "foul apples" and fix the "rotten barrel."
(v) Continuous training and development for employees led to better outcomes at the PPWSA and enabled the evaluation of staff.

Political legitimacy
(i) Top-down political intent to engage in reform for tangible change was necessary.
(ii) Government support was essential, for example to increase financial autonomy, allow increased tariffs, and provide the initial capital investment.
(iii) A political "rapport" was necessary to secure support and protect from interference.

Source: A. K. Biswas and C. Trotajada. 2009. *Water Supply of Phnom Penh: A Most Remarkable Transformation.* Atizapán, Mexico: Third World Centre for Water Management/Zaragoza, Spain: International Centre for Water.

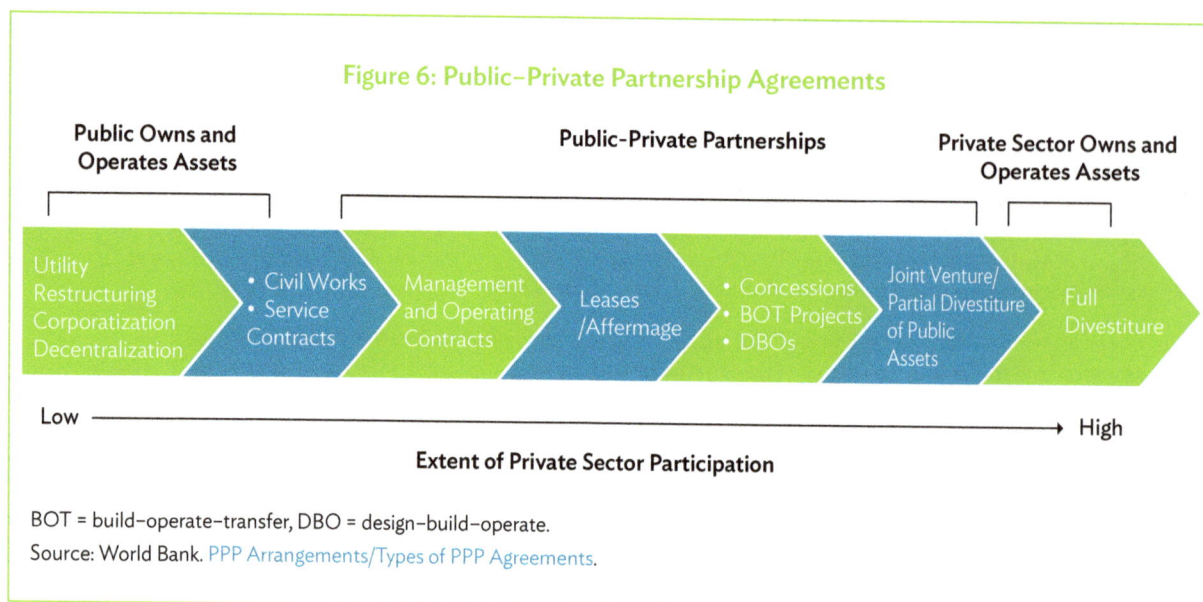

Figure 6: Public–Private Partnership Agreements

BOT = build–operate–transfer, DBO = design–build–operate.
Source: World Bank. PPP Arrangements/Types of PPP Agreements.

However, setting up JVs or other forms of PPPs requires the SOE to provide relevant resources, such as knowledge, physical assets, etc., to make it attractive for the private partner to join the JV. The SOE in the JV also needs to be able to make autonomous decisions based on the JV contract on mostly or fully commercial terms. This often requires the SOE to overcome specific governance issues. For example, some SOE staff may be seconded to the JV, which has different salary and hierarchy structures, and the SOE needs to find ways to deal with this.

To further improve the bankability of a specific bond issuance, SOEs or the PPP can utilize a number of **debt enhancement mechanisms**. These include blended finance mechanisms that utilize both commercial and concessionary finance to reduce the overall financing cost (Figure 7).

Additionally, SOEs can work with strong and credible **anchor investors and underwriters** before floating the green bond on the market, for example through multilateral development banks, policy banks, or even private investors. These investors provide credibility and assurance for other public investors.

Ensuring "Greenness" through Domestic and International Standards

Once the governance and bankability prerequisites for SOE green bond issuance are met, the actual process of green bond issuance starts. ADB published detailed guidance for SOE green bond issuances in December 2021. Figure 8 presents the relevant steps for the SOE green bond issuance process (for a more detailed description, see ADB's *Detailed Guidance for Issuing Green Bonds in Developing Countries*).[34]

One key issue in the green bond issuance involves ensuring that the use of proceeds is appropriately described in the legal documentation for security purposes; therefore, all designated green projects should provide clear and defined environmental benefits. Accordingly, the issuer will assess and, where feasible, quantify the environmental benefits. The SOE needs to clearly specify if parts of the bond are used for refinancing.

---

[34]   ADB. 2021. *Detailed Guidance for Issuing Green Bonds in Developing Countries*. Manila.

Figure 7: Blended Finance Mechanism

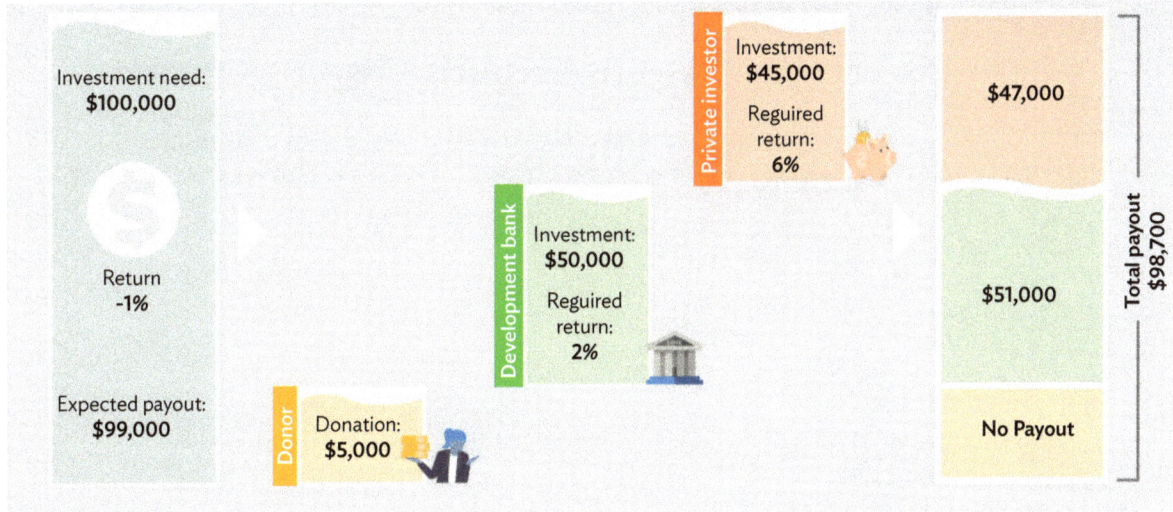

Investment need:
$100,000

Return
-1%

Expected payout:
$99,000

Donor
Donation:
$5,000

Development bank
Investment:
$50,000

Required
return:
2%

Private investor
Investment:
$45,000

Required
return:
6%

$47,000

$51,000

No Payout

Total payout
$98,700

Source: C. Nedopil Wang and Q. Xu. 2020. *Technical Report on SDG Finance Taxonomy (China)*. Beijing: United Nations Development Programme..

Figure 8: Outline of Green Bond Issuance

Identifying green projects and assets → Developing a green bond and sustainable finance framework → Confirming internal processes and controls → Reporting on allocations and green credentials ↓

Media, stakeholders, indexes and listings ← Seeking certification or recognition ← Managing the external review process ← Setting up for impact reporting

↓
Post-issuance reporting and disclosure → Further issuance of labeled instruments

Source: Asian Development Bank. 2021. *Detailed Guidance for Issuing Green Bonds in Developing Countries*. Manila.

To attract international investors, external opinions on the green bond are particularly encouraged. These can be divided into

(i)   **second-party opinion** to confirm alignment with the green bond framework (objectives, strategy, governance);

(ii) **verification** to evaluate the issuance against designated green bond criteria, including stated environmental impacts;

(iii) **certification** to certify the bond against the recognized green bond standard; and

(iv) **scoring** to assess the bond's key features against those of other issuers to provide a relative score.

4 Support Measures to Accelerate State-Owned Enterprise Green Bond Issuances

On their journey to issue green bonds and apply green finance more broadly, SOEs can benefit from various direct and indirect support measures. These measures can address the three major ingredients of a successful SOE green bond issuance. Direct measures improve (i) the corporate governance and (ii) the bankability and greenness of the SOE; whereas, indirect measures improve (iii) the enabling environment.

Direct Support Measures for State-Owned Enterprises by Development Partners

SOEs can be supported directly at a company level by external parties, such as development finance institutions. These measures can include, among others, the following:

(i)   technical assistance to develop a green bond framework; improve corporate governance including risk management processes, transparency, and reporting; or develop green project pipelines;

(ii)   facilitation funds to support the evaluation and design of green projects and their implementation, similar to the ASEAN Catalytic Green Facility;

(iii)   technical assistance or facilitation funds to compensate for costs associated with developing and verifying the green bond framework; green bond issuance; and measurement, reporting, and validation;

(iv)   technical assistance or facilitation funds to support credit ratings (which are independent of green verification) on the SOE or issuing company (e.g., PPP);

(v)   provision or mobilization of anchor investments in green bonds to reduce risks and signal credibility of the bond to external investors (e.g., the Georgia railway green bond issuance presented in Box 4);

(vi)   provision of equity injections to provide further space for debt issuances; and

(vii)   foreign exchange risk reduction facilities to compensate international investors for foreign exchange risks in local currency bond issuances.

A particular focus in countries with less developed capital markets and less developed SOEs should be support to state-owned financial institutions. These financial institutions can serve as an intermediary between capital markets and provide green loans to commercial clients. In this case, relevant capacities for the development of a green credit strategy and framework, green credit evaluation, and management need to be provided to the Board and relevant loan departments.

Box 4: Anchor Investment to Support Georgia Railway Green Bond Issuance

In June 2021, Georgia Railway issued a $500 million green bond on the London Stock Exchange to refinance a maturing Eurobond issued in July 2012. Georgia Railway is owned by JSC Partnership Fund, a state-owned investment fund in Georgia.

Several factors allowed Georgia Railway to issue the green bond:

(i)   Georgia Railway already had capital market exposure and experience through previous bond issuances.
(ii)   Georgia Railway developed a green bond framework,[a] published in May 2021. Within that framework, Georgia Railway specified the use of proceeds, example projects, and impact metrics; it linked to relevant SDGs and a detailed process for evaluation, environmental risk management, management of proceeds, reporting, and external review.
(iii)   The green bond framework was audited by S&P Global, which found it aligned with the four components of the Green Bond Principles 2018.[b]
(iv)   The bond itself received a BB- rating from Fitch.[c]
(v)   Georgia Railway gained the support of multilateral development banks to serve as anchor investors, providing at least 14% of the original investment: the Asian Development Bank invested $20 million, as it complements ongoing technical assistance to Georgian Railway to strengthen its planning for passenger services;[d] and the European Bank for Reconstruction and Development invested $50 million.[e]

The green bond ended up being eight times oversubscribed.[f] It also has a significantly lower interest rate, at 4.0% for a period of 7 years, compared with the previous bond at 7.75%. This brings savings of about $20 million per year for Georgia Railway. This was the first green bond issued by Georgia Railway, and the first transport-related green bond from the Caucasus region.

Georgia Railway is owned by JSC Partnership Fund, a state-owned investment fund in Georgia.

———————————————

[a]   JSC Georgian Railway. 2021. Green Bond Framework. Tbilisi: JSC Georgian Railway.
[b]   S&P Global. 2021. Georgian Railway Green Bond Framework. Green Framework Alignment Opinion. 26 May. Paris, New York: S&P Global.
[c]   FitchRatings. 2021. Fitch Assigns Georgian Railway's USD500m Green Bond Final 'BB-' Rating. 16 June.
[d]   ADB. 2021. ADB Invests $20 Million in Georgian Railway Green Bonds to Modernize Rail Network. News release. 18 June.
[e]   EBRD. 2021. SC Georgian Railway Green Bond.
[f]   O. Batrak. 2021. Demand for 500 Million Georgian Railway Green Bonds Exceeds $ 4 Billion. Railway Supply. 25 June.

Indirect Support Measures to Improve the Enabling Environment for State-Owned Enterprise Green Bond Issuances

In addition to direct support for SOEs, support can be given at a system level to improve green capital market development, support the government in SOE management and governance, and address "real economy" barriers and bottlenecks to green transition. This includes addressing gaps in the enforcement of environmental regulation and the pricing of negative externalities such as carbon emissions through carbon prices (e.g., carbon tax, emission trading schemes), which should accelerate the demand for green investment.

Government entities, including the ministry and/or regulator responsible for SOEs, the capital market regulator, capital markets directly, and ministries responsible for environmental regulation and banking (particularly the development of green credit) can support the adoption of green finance by

(i)   addressing real economic barriers through **developing binding environmental regulation**, emission trading schemes, or other policies that help internalize negative externalities (footnote 15);

(ii)   **setting policy frameworks for green transition** through road maps and binding regulations (e.g., climate targets) to signal to private and public companies future investment directions;

(iii)   **developing local capital market capacity and structures**, including green finance frameworks and disclosure frameworks (ESG) that are attractive and trustworthy to international investors;

(iv)   **improving SOE governance and the SOE management regulatory environment**, including the autonomy of SOEs to raise funds, regulatory aspects of bankability, transparency, and disclosure;

(v)   **developing green banking capacity** for the responsible banking regulator to provide green credit frameworks, including green credit statistics frameworks—e.g., the Sustainable Banking and Finance Network (formerly the Sustainable Banking Network) is supporting such capacity building in 62 countries by working with banking regulators and banking associations; and

(vi)   **providing support to PPP capacity** to accelerate private sector funding for critical infrastructure projects by structuring viable and bankable projects through transaction advisory services—similar to the cooperation with Indonesia's PT Sarana Multi Infrastruktur.

5 Conclusion and Outlook

The green transition of SOEs is paramount to meet global climate goals and avoid catastrophic climate change. As SOEs, particularly in Asian countries, play a central role in many of the high-emitting sectors such as energy and transport, they need to mobilize billions of (United States) dollars to invest in new assets, while reducing reliance on high-emitting and inefficient assets (e.g., coal-fired power plants) as quickly as possible. As government funds for this transition have become difficult to mobilize—not least because of a tense sovereign debt situation—SOEs must find ways to use the growing toolbox of green and sustainable finance instruments. Green bonds, in particular, can serve as important tools to mobilize private sector capital for green transition. Currently, however, SOEs have much untapped potential in the green bond and green financial markets— because of governance, bankability, and green eligibility issues. SOEs that successfully utilize the green finance toolbox can provide relatively large bond issuances at potentially lower risk that are particularly interesting for global investors.

However, as this report shows, to utilize green bonds (and other sustainable finance instruments), most SOEs must improve their corporate governance to attract investors, while also building capacity to issue green bonds according to domestic and/or international standards. Greening SOEs through green finance requires cooperation between the owners of the SOEs (various ministries, government agencies, and holding companies), their regulators, local capital markets, and the SOEs themselves. Role models of successful SOE green bond issuances should provide an impetus for other SOEs. Successful utilization of green bonds will ultimately support the upgrading of SOEs and whole economies to generate a greener, more resilient future.

APPENDIX 1
Regulatory Approaches to Green Finance Standards

Country	Standard	Established	Secretariat	Description
PRC	Green Bond Endorsed Projects Catalogue	First in December 2015 Latest version in April 2021	People's Bank of China, NDRC, and China Securities Regulatory Commission	The People's Bank of China (PRC's central bank) released the first country-specific green bond issuance guidelines along with a taxonomy in the form of the Green Bond Endorsed Projects Catalogue to guide financial sector issuance on green bonds in the PRC.[a]
	Guidance on Green Bond Issuance	Issued in December 2015 No updated version so far	NDRC	The NDRC released the Guidance on Green Bond Issuance, which encourages green bond issuance.[b]
	Guiding Catalogue for Green Industries	Released in March 2019	NDRC with other ministries	The NDRC led six ministries to jointly issue the Guiding Catalogue for Green Industries and related instructions to assist other policymakers in formulating relevant guidelines for green financing products, including green bonds.[c] It includes the use of "clean coal" and is particularly applicable to corporate issuers.
India	Disclosure Requirements for Issuance and Listing of Green Debt Securities	Issued in May 2017	SEBI	In May 2017, the SEBI issued the final rules that will govern the issuance of green bonds locally. These include a list of broad project and asset categories for eligible use of proceeds.

continued on next page

Appendix 1 table *continued*

Country	Standard	Established	Secretariat	Description
EU	EUGBS	EU Taxonomy first released in 2019, agreed to in 2022 on which the EUGBS followed	Technical Expert Group on Sustainable Finance	The EUGBS is a voluntary standard to help scale up and raise the environmental ambitions of the green bond market. Establishing this standard was an action in the Commission's 2018 action plan on financing sustainable growth and is part of the European green deal.[d] It focuses on renewable energy (solar and wind), energy-efficient buildings, public transport, etc.

EU = European Union, EUGBS = European green bond standard, NDRC = National Development and Reform Commission, PRC = People's Republic of China, SEBI = Securities and Exchange Board of India.

[a] People's Bank of China, NDRC, and China Securities Regulatory Commission. 2021. *Green Bond Endorsed Projects Catalogue (2021 Edition).* Beijing.
[b] General Office of the NDRC. 2015. *Notice of the General Office of the National Development and Reform Commission on Printing and Distributing the "Guidelines for the Issuance of Green Bonds."* China Bond. 31 December.
[c] China Banking Association. 2020. *Guiding Catalogue for Green Industries (2019 Edition)* (in Chinese).
[d] European Commission. *European Green Bond Standard.*

APPENDIX 2
International Green Bond Standards

Standard	Established	Secretariat	Description	Application	Core Component
Green Bond Principles	First drafted in early 2014 Published in March 2015 Latest version in June 2021	ICMA	The GBP are a set of voluntary guidelines aimed at promoting transparency and disclosure for green bonds. They have achieved broad market acceptance and legitimacy, as well as growing official recognition by policymakers and regulators.[a]	Renewable energy Energy efficiency Pollution prevention and control Environmentally sustainable management of living natural resources and land use Terrestrial and aquatic biodiversity conservation Clean transportation Sustainable water and wastewater management Climate change adaptation Circular economy adapted products, production technologies, and processes Green buildings that meet regional, national, or internationally recognized standards or certifications for environmental performance	1. Use of proceeds 2. Process for project evaluation and selection 3. Management of proceeds 4. Reporting

continued on next page

Appendix 2 table *continued*

Standard	Established	Secretariat	Description	Application	Core Component
ASEAN Green Bond Standards	First issued in November 2017 Latest version in October 2018	ACMF	The ASEAN GBS is an initiative that facilitates ASEAN capital markets in tapping green finance to support sustainable regional growth and meet investor interest for green investments. It is part of the ACMF's broader efforts in developing green finance for the region.[b]	Renewable energy Energy efficiency Pollution prevention and control Environmentally sustainable management of living natural resources and land use Terrestrial and aquatic biodiversity conservation Clean transportation Sustainable water and wastewater management Climate change adaptation Eco-efficient and/or circular-economy-adapted products, production technologies, and processes Green buildings that meet regional, national, or internationally recognized standards or certifications	1. Use of proceeds 2. Process for project evaluation and selection 3. Management of proceeds 4. Reporting
ASEAN Taxonomy for Sustainable Finance	First issued in November 2021 No revisions as of data	ASEAN Taxonomy Board	The ASEAN Taxonomy is an overarching guide that caters to the different ASEAN economies, financial systems, and transition paths. It is conceived as a multitiered	Agriculture, forestry, and fishing Manufacturing Electricity, gas, steam, and air-conditioning supply	1. Taxonomy design and considerations 2. Environmental objectives and essential criteria 3. Sector coverage

continued on next page

Appendix 2 table *continued*

Standard	Established	Secretariat	Description	Application	Core Component
			framework that takes into account those differences among member states. The adopted criteria essential for the economic activities are aimed at achieving those objectives in the most transparent manner. Among the most important criteria are "do no significant harm" and existence of remedial efforts to transition.[c]	Transportation and storage Construction and real estate activities Water supply, sewerage, waste management, and remediation activities	4. Classification approach
Climate Bonds Standard	Version 1.0 revised May 2015 Latest version in December 2019	CBI	CBI is an international organization working to mobilize global capital for climate action. As of end of June 2017, the CBS, which was released in its second version in December 2015, represents the broadest internationally recognized green or climate bond certification scheme.[d]	NA	1. Use of proceeds 2. Process for project evaluation and selection 3. Management of proceeds 4. Reporting

ACMF = ASEAN Capital Markets Forum, ASEAN = Association of Southeast Asian Nations, CBI = Climate Bonds Initiative, CBS = Climate Bonds Standard, GBP = Green Bond Principles, GBS = Green Bond Standards, ICMA = International Capital Markets Association, NA = not applicable.

[a] ICMA. 2021. *Green Bond Principles: Voluntary Process Guidelines for Issuing Green Bonds.* Paris.
[b] ASEAN Capital Markets Forum (ACMF). 2018. *ASEAN Green Bond Standards.* Phnom Penh.
[c] ASEAN Taxonomy Board. 2021. *ASEAN Taxonomy for Sustainable Finance.* Jakarta: The ASEAN Secretariat.
[d] Climate Bonds Initiative (CBI). 2021. *How to Issue Green Bonds, Social Bonds, and Sustainability Bonds.* London: CBI / Hanoi: State Securities Commission of Vietnam.

References

Almond, R. E. A., M. Grooten, and T. Petersen, eds. 2020. *Living Planet Report 2020: Bending the Curve of Biodiversity Loss*. Gland, Switzerland: WWF.

Asian Development Bank (ADB). 2017. *Meeting Asia's Infrastructure Needs*. Manila.

_____. 2021. *ADB Green Bond Newsletter and Impact Report*. Manila.

_____. *2021.* ADB Invests $20 Million in Georgian Railway Green Bonds to Modernize Rail Network. News release. *18 June.*

_____. 2021. *Detailed Guidance for Issuing Green Bonds in Developing Countries*. Manila.

_____. 2021. *Guidance Note on State-Owned Enterprise Reform in Sovereign Projects and Programs*. Manila.

_____. 2021. *The Bankable SOE: Commercial Financing for State-Owned Enterprises*. Manila.

_____. *2022.* ADB Supports Thailand's First Social Bond Issued by State-Owned Government Savings Bank. News release. *29 June.*

Association of Southeast Asian Nations (ASEAN) Capital Markets Forum (ACMF). 2018. *ASEAN Green Bond Standards. Phnom Penh.*

_____. *2018. ASEAN Social Bond Standards. Phnom Penh.*

_____. *2020. Roadmap for ASEAN Sustainable Capital Markets*. Phnom Penh.

ASEAN Taxonomy Board. 2021. *ASEAN Taxonomy for Sustainable Finance*. Jakarta: The ASEAN Secretariat.

Bancel, F. and D. Glavas. 2017. *The Role of State Ownership as a Determinant of Green Bond Issuance*. Rochester, NY: Social Science Research Network.

Biswas, A. K. and C. Trotajada. 2009. *Water Supply of Phnom Penh: A Most Remarkable Transformation*. Atizapán, Mexico: Third World Centre for Water Management / Zaragoza, Spain: International Centre for Water.

China Banking Association. 2020. *Guiding Catalogue for Green Industries* (2019 Edition) (in Chinese).

Clark, A. and P. Benoit. 2022. Greenhouse Gas Emissions from State-Owned Enterprises: A Preliminary Inventory. *Center on Global Energy Policy*. 3 February.

Climate Bonds Initiative (CBI). Explaining Green Bonds.

_____. Interactive Data Platform (accessed 18 May 2022).

_____. 2021. *How to Issue Green Bonds, Social Bonds, and Sustainability Bonds.* London: CBI / Hanoi: State Securities Commission of Vietnam.

Climate Bonds Initiative. 2022. Certified Green Issuance Passes $200bn – Expansion of Climate Bonds Standard in 2022: Basic Chemicals, Cement, Steel in Pipeline. 11 January.

Darcy, J. and T. Kelly. 2015. *Green Bonds: Emergence of the Australian and Asian Markets.* Melbourne: Allens / Hong Kong, China: Linklaters.

Engel, H. et al. 2020. Low-Carbon Economic Stimulus after COVID-19. McKinsey Global Institute.

European Bank for Reconstruction and Development. SC Georgian Railway Green Bond (approved 9 June 2021).

European Commission. European Green Bond Standard.

European Investment Bank. 2021. *Key Findings – Evaluation of the EIB's Climate Awareness Bonds.* Luxembourg.

Fitch Ratings. 2021. Fitch Assigns Georgian Railway's USD500m Green Bond Final 'BB-' Rating. Rating Action Commentary. 16 June.

General Office of the National Development and Reform Commission. 2015. *Notice of the General Office of the National Development and Reform Commission on Printing and Distributing the "Guidelines for the Issuance of Green Bonds."* China Bond. 31 December.

International Capital Markets Association (ICMA). 2021. *Green Bond Principles: Voluntary Process Guidelines for Issuing Green Bonds.* Paris.

International Energy Agency. Share of State-Owned Energy Investments by Economy Type and Sector, 2019 (accessed 3 May 2022).

International Finance Corporation. 2019. *Corporate Governance of State-Owned Enterprises.* Washington, DC.

International Renewable Energy Agency (IRENA) and ASEAN Centre for Energy (ACE). 2022. *Renewable Energy Outlook for ASEAN: Towards a Regional Energy Transition* (2nd edition). Abu Dhabi: IRENA / Jakarta: ACE.

JSC Georgian Railway. 2021. *Green Bond Framework.* Tbilisi.

Lazard. 2021. Levelized Cost of Energy, Levelized Cost of Storage, and Levelized Cost of Hydrogen. 28 October.

Münzer-Jones, V. and D. Johnson. 2016. *Recent Developments in the Asian Green Bond Markets.* Norton Rose Fulbright.

Nedopil Wang, C. 2022. *Coal Phase-Out in the Belt and Road Initiative (BRI): An Analysis of Chinese-Backed Coal Power from 2014-2020.* Beijing: Green BRI Center, International Institute of Green Finance.

_____. 2022. State-Owned Enterprises and Asia's Energy Transition. *East Asia Forum Quarterly*. 14 (2). pp. 19–21.

Nedopil Wang, C. and Q. Xu. 2020. *Technical Report on SDG Finance Taxonomy (China)*. Beijing: United Nations Development Programme.

Network for Greening the Financial System. 2019. *A Call for Action: Climate Change as a Source of Financial Risk*. Paris.

Organisation for Economic Co-operation and Development (OECD). 2015. *OECD Guidelines on Corporate Governance of State-Owned Enterprises*. 2015 Edition. Paris.

_____. 2018. Energy Sector SOEs: You Have the Power! *OECD on the Level*. 19 April.

People's Bank of China, National Development and Reform Commission, and China Securities Regulatory Commission. 2021. *Green Bond Endorsed Projects Catalogue (2021 Edition)*. Beijing.

Railway Supply. 2021. Demand for 500 Million Georgian Railway Green Bonds Exceeds $4 Billion. 25 June.

Robinett, D. 2020. Reform State-Owned Enterprises to Avoid a COVID-19 Debt and Investment Crisis. Asian Development Blog. 3 June.

S&P Global Ratings. 2021. Georgian Railway Green Bond Framework. *Green Framework Alignment Opinion*. 26 May.

Securities and Exchange Board of India. 2017. Disclosure Requirements for Issuance and Listing of Green Debt Securities. *Circular No. CIR/IMD/DF/51/2017. 30 May.*

Shen, S., A. Galbraith, and T. Westbrook. 2020. China's Bond Defaults Show Beijing's War on Debt Is Back. *Reuters*. 25 November.

Volz, U. 2018. Fostering Green Finance for Sustainable Development in Asia. *ADBI Working Paper Series*. No. 814. Tokyo: Asian Development Bank Institute.

Wong, S. 2018. The State of Governance at State-Owned Enterprises. *Private Sector Opinion*. Issue 40. Washington, DC: International Finance Corporation.

Zhou, X., C. Wilson, and B. Caldecott. 2021. *The Energy Transition and Changing Financing Costs*. Oxford: University of Oxford.

www.ingramcontent.com/pod-product-compliance
Lightning Source LLC
Chambersburg PA
CBHW050056220326
41599CB00045B/7432